THE HISTORY DETECTIVE INVESTIGATES

Monarchs

Simon Adams

The History Detective Investigates series:
The Celts
Anglo-Saxons
Tudor Exploration
Tudor Home
Tudor Medicine
Tudor Theatre
Tudor War
The Civil Wars
Victorian Crime
Victorian Factory
Victorian School
Victorian Transport
Local History
The Industrial Revolution
Post-War Britain
The Normans and the Battle of Hastings
Monarchs
Weapons and Armour through the Ages
Castles

First published in paperback in 2015 by Wayland

Dewey Number: 305.5'22-dc22
ISBN: 978-0-7502-9425-6
Library eBook ISBN: 978-0-7502-7353-4
10 9 8 7 6 5 4 3 2 1

Editor: David John
Designer: Darren Jordan
Consultant: Andy Robertshaw

Wayland
An imprint of
Hachette Children's Group
Part of Hodder & Stoughton
Carmelite House
50 Victoria Embankment
London EC4Y 0DZ

Printed in Malaysia

An Hachette UK company
www.hachette.co.uk
www.hachettechildrens.co.uk

Picture Acknowledgments: Front cover left Duncan1890/iStockphoto.com; front cover right Bettmann/Corbis; 1 Getty Images; 2 iStockphoto.com; 4t Roland Nagy/Dreamstime.com; 5bl C Squared Studios; 5br Anthony Baggett/Dreamstime.com; 7t Hulton Archive; 7b MHardcastle/GNU Creative Commons ShareAlike; 8b William McKelvie/Dreamstime.com; 9tr The Bridgeman Art Library; 9br Scubabartek/Dreamstime.com; 10b Mikule/Dreamstime.com; 11t The Bridgeman Art Library; 12b Albertistvan/GNU ShareAlike; 13t iStockphoto.com; 13b GNU ShareAlike; 16b The Bridgeman Art Library; 18t Creativehearts/Dreamstime.com; 21t Time & Life Pictures; 21b Hulton Archive/Handout; 24t Ejdzej/Creative Commons ShareAlike; 25t English School; 26t Diliff/Dreamstime.com; 27b Courtesy of NASA; 29t iStockphoto.com.

Above: Edward I was king of England from 1272 to 1307.
Previous page: The coronation of Elizabeth II took place in 1953.

Contents

What is a monarch?	4
Who was the first king of England?	6
When did Scotland first have a king?	8
Who was the first Norman king?	10
Why does Wales have a prince?	12
What were the Wars of the Roses?	14
Why did Henry VIII marry six times?	16
Who united the crowns?	18
Why did a king lose his head?	20
When did the kings speak German?	22
Which monarch reigned the longest?	24
Why is the royal family named after a castle?	26
Your project	28
Glossary	30
Answers	31
Further Information	31
Index	32

Words in **bold** can be found in the glossary on page 30.

 The history detective Sherlock Bones will help you to find clues and collect evidence about monarchs. Wherever you see one of Sherlock's paw-prints, you will find a mystery to solve. The answers can be found on page 31.

What is a monarch?

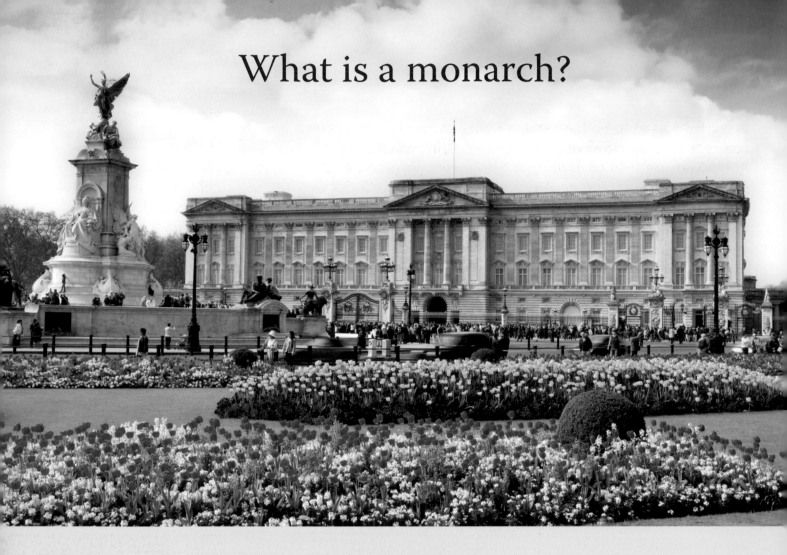

The United Kingdom of Great Britain and Northern Ireland – the official name of the country we live in – is a monarchy. That means the United Kingdom is ruled by a monarch known as a king or queen. But what is a monarch, and what does he or she do?

A **monarch** is a person who rules a country known as a **kingdom**. If that monarch rules more than one country or kingdom, he or she is called an emperor or empress and rules an **empire**. A new monarch is crowned at a ceremony called a **coronation**. The monarch's main role is head of state. That means he – and it usually is a he, as women monarchs are much less common – is a symbol and **figurehead** of their country. In the past, monarchs were not only head of state but also head of government. They ran the country, commanded the armed services, approved new laws, and controlled everything that went on in the country. Today, most monarchs have handed day-to-day power over to a separate head of government, usually called a prime minister.

Buckingham Palace in London has been the official home of the British monarch since 1837.

🐾 **What is worn by a monarch during a coronation ceremony and other state occasions?**

Monarchy used to be the most common form of government across the world. However, some countries, including ancient Rome, were **republics**. That means they were governed by a person chosen by some or all of the adult population. Today, most countries in the world, including the USA, France and Germany, are republics. Monarchies or their equivalents survive in Britain, Belgium, the Netherlands, Scandinavia, Spain and some African and Asian nations, such as Morocco, Thailand and Saudi Arabia. Fifteen countries once ruled by Britain, including Canada and Australia, still have the British queen as their head of state.

Britain, as the United Kingdom is commonly known, has been a monarchy ever since it was created. The term British Isles, confusingly, includes the whole of Ireland, but only Northern Ireland is part of the United Kingdom. Great Britain is the island that comprises England, Wales and Scotland. These were once independent from each other, with their own monarchies. Over the centuries, they became united and they now share a monarch.

DETECTIVE WORK

Kings and queens have ruled England for almost 1,200 years, and England and Scotland have been part of the same monarchy for the last 400 years. Find out more about them at www. britannia.com/history /h6f.html

Monarchs belong to a **dynasty** or royal **house** or family. When a monarch dies, his or her **heir** – usually the eldest **prince** or son but sometimes a princess or daughter – becomes the new monarch. This system of handing the monarchy down through the generations is known as the **hereditary system**.

The Imperial State Crown of the British monarch contains diamonds, sapphires, emeralds and rubies.

Westminster Abbey in London is where British monarchs are crowned and also where they are buried.

Who was the first king of England?

The story of the kings of England begins after 409 CE, when the last Roman soldiers – who had occupied England for nearly 400 years – left the country. Britannia, as the Romans called their province of England and Wales, now came under attack from Angles, Saxons and Jutes from northern Germany. The invaders set up their own small kingdoms.

By the early 600s, England comprised seven rival Anglo-Saxon kingdoms: Kent, Sussex, Essex, East Anglia, Wessex, Mercia and Northumbria. Cornwall, Wales and Scotland, which had only partly been occupied by the Romans, and Ireland, which had never been Roman, were split between many small kingdoms and **princedoms**.

🐾 **What types of precious goods did Anglo-Saxon kings like to be buried with?**

FORTRIU

STRATHCLYDE

NORTHUMBRIA

BRITAIN

GWYNEDD

POWYS

MERCIA

EAST ANGLIA

DYFED

GWENT

ESSEX

WESSEX

KENT

SUSSEX

DUMNONIA

DETECTIVE WORK

The seventh-century Anglo-Saxon kings of East Anglia buried their dead at Sutton Hoo in modern-day Suffolk. Finds there include a helmet, shield, silverware and spoons. To learn more about the treasures, visit www.nationaltrust.org.uk/main/w-suttonhoo

When Ecgberht became king of Wessex in 802, Britain was divided into several different kingdoms and princedoms. The most powerful of these were Northumbria, Wessex and Mercia.

This painting shows the defeat in 878 of the Viking longships by Alfred's navy, at Swanage in modern-day Dorset.

At first, Northumbria was the most powerful English kingdom, followed by Mercia. But after the death of Offa, king of Mercia in 796, Wessex gained the upper hand. In 802, Ecgberht became king of Wessex. He defeated the Mercians in battle in 825 and forced Northumbria to submit to him in 829. The various kings of England then proclaimed him 'Bretwalda' or 'king of all England'. Thus Ecgberht became England's first king until his death in 839.

Ecgberht's grandson, Alfred, ruled Wessex from 871 to 899. The union of the kingdoms created by Ecgberht had already fallen apart and England was being invaded by Vikings from Norway and Denmark. In 878, Alfred defeated the Viking leader and signed a treaty with him, dividing England in two along a line from London to Chester. Alfred ruled south of the line. The Vikings ruled Danelaw to the north. In 886 Alfred captured London and was accepted by both Anglo-Saxons and Vikings as king of all England. Alfred created the first permanent English navy and ordered the writing of the *Anglo-Saxon Chronicle*, a record of important events. He is the only English king to be known as 'the Great'.

'[Alfred] came to a place called Edington, and with a close shield-wall fought fiercely against the whole army of [the Vikings]; his attack was long and spirited, and finally by divine aid he triumphed and overthrew [the Vikings] with a very great slaughter… [The Vikings] sought a peace by which the king was to take from them as many named hostages as he wished while he gave none to them – a kind of peace that they had never before concluded with any one… [The Vikings] took oath that they would most speedily leave his kingdom, and also Guthrum, their king, promised to accept Christianity and to receive baptism at the hands of King Alfred.'

Bishop Asser wrote in 893 about Alfred's defeat of the Viking king Guthrum in 878.

This gold buckle was found at Sutton Hoo, Suffolk, a burial site for East Anglian kings.

When did Scotland first have a king?

Just as the kingdom of England was formed out of warring kingdoms, so too was Scotland. From the sixth to the ninth century, Scotland was made up of four separate kingdoms: Dalraida in the west, the kingdom of the Pictish peoples in the north, Bernicia in Lothian in the east, and Strathclyde in the southwest.

In 843, Kenneth MacAlpin, the king of Dalraida, defeated the Pictish kingdom, uniting the two kingdoms under his leadership. Although he did not unite the whole of Scotland, he is considered to be the first true king of Scotland.

Kenneth's descendant Malcolm II defeated a Viking and English army at Carham in 1018 and brought Lothian into his kingdom. A year later, Strathclyde joined the kingdom. Malcolm now ruled a kingdom with much the same borders as modern Scotland has today. Although Scotland was now united and independent, its fate was always tied up with its powerful neighbour, England.

In April 1320, 51 Scottish lords and bishops met at Arbroath and wrote a letter to Pope John XXII asking him to recognise Scotland's independence:

'For, as long as but a hundred of us remain alive, never will we on any conditions be brought under English rule. It is in truth not for glory, nor riches, nor honours that we are fighting, but for freedom – for that alone, which no honest man gives up but with life itself.'

DETECTIVE WORK

Apart from brief periods of English rule, Scotland was governed by Scottish kings and queens for more than 850 years. To learn the names of all the Scottish monarchs, visit www.edinburgh-royalmile.com/castle/kingsandqueens.html

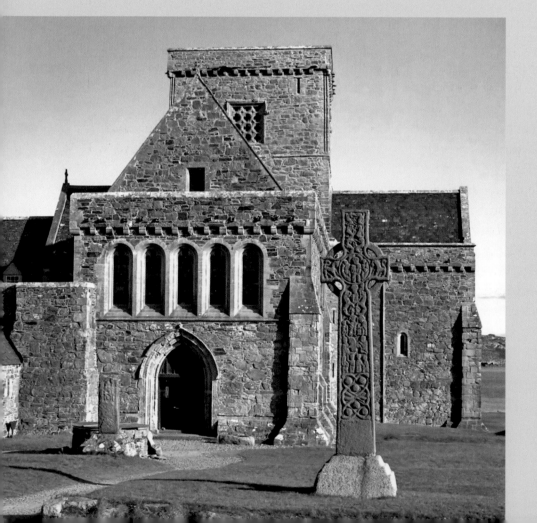

As many as 48 Scottish kings are buried at Iona Abbey (left) on the Isle of Iona, off the western coast of Scotland. Kenneth MacAlpin, Scotland's first king, lies there.

In 1040, Duncan I of Scotland invaded England but was pushed back and then killed in a **civil war**. In 1072, William I of England, 'the Conqueror', invaded Scotland and forced Malcolm III to recognise him as his **overlord**.

Malcolm invaded England and he was also killed. In 1173–74, another Scottish king, William the Lyon, invaded England but was captured by Henry I and forced to surrender Scottish independence to him.

This constant battle between England and Scotland reached its climax in 1290, when Margaret, the six-year-old queen of Scotland, died without an heir. The Scottish nobles asked the English king, Edward I, to choose a king for them. In 1294, Edward's choice, John Balliol, refused to join him on a campaign in France, so Edward invaded Scotland and from 1296 ruled Scotland himself.

The first Scot to rebel against English rule, William Wallace, was killed by the English in 1305. The next Scot, Robert Bruce, took on Wallace's role and in 1306 was crowned Robert I of Scotland. In 1314, he defeated the English army, led by Edward II, at Bannockburn outside Stirling. Fighting between the two countries continued until, in 1328, a new English king, Edward III, recognised Robert as king and Scotland as an independent nation. Scotland remained independent until 1707.

Robert Bruce (shown here with his wife Isabella) was crowned king of Scotland in 1306.

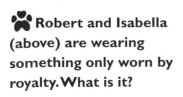

Robert and Isabella (above) are wearing something only worn by royalty. What is it?

William Wallace, the Scottish rebel, is celebrated in a statue at Edinburgh Castle.

Who was the first Norman king?

In 1066, a warlike people known as the Normans invaded England from northern France. The Normans were descendants of the Vikings – raiders from Scandinavia who had terrorised the coasts of Britain for about 300 years. At various times they had occupied large parts of the country, and had even ruled the whole country for a time during the eleventh century.

In 911, a group of Vikings raided the northern coast of France. The French king, Charles the Simple, gave them their own land in the hope they would stop raiding his country. The land became known as Northmannia, 'the land of the Northmen', a name later simplified to Normandy.

When the Vikings arrived in France, they spoke their own language and were **pagans**. Over time, they intermarried with the French, whose language they adopted, and converted to Christianity. In 1035, control of Normandy passed to an **illegitimate** boy, William. He became a skilled military commander.

William the Conqueror was a keen hunter, and enclosed the New Forest in southern England as a royal hunting area. The historian William of Malmesbury, born at the end of William's reign, described him:

'Of just stature, ordinary corpulence, fierce countenance; his forehead was bare of hair; of such great strength of arm that it was often a matter of surprise, that no one was able to draw his bow, which himself could bend when his horse was in full gallop; he was majestic whether sitting or standing, although the protuberance of his belly deformed his royal person; of excellent health … so given to the pleasures of the chase.'

William the Conqueror built York Castle (left) on top of a man-made mound, or motte, as part of his plan to bring northern England under his control.

HIC·DVX·VVILGELM·CVM HAROLDO·VE
LAT

Links between Normandy and England were strong, as the English king, Edward the Confessor (reigned 1042–66), had lived in Normandy as a child. Edward promised the English **crown** to William, but as he lay dying in January 1066, he changed his mind and the crown passed to his brother-in-law, Harold.

William was furious and prepared to invade England to claim his **throne**. While Harold was in the north of England defeating a large Viking army at Stamford Bridge, William landed in Sussex. Harold hurried south, and on 14 October 1066 the two armies met a few miles north of Hastings. The battle could have gone either way until William's troops pretended to run away. As Harold's army pursued them, the Normans turned round and killed the English troops, including Harold.

The crown of England now belonged to William. As the first Norman king of England, he transformed the country until his death in 1087. Norman lords took over the lands of the defeated English, and the peasants were forced to give unpaid service to these new lords.

The Bayeux Tapestry, which dates from around 1070, shows Harold and William (on the black horse) a few years before the Norman invasion.

🐾 **In the picture above, what is William carrying and why?**

DETECTIVE WORK

The four Norman kings ruled England from 1066 to 1154 and greatly changed the country. Find out more about the Normans and their lives on www.historyonthenet.com/Normans/normansmain.htm

Why does Wales have a prince?

Much like England and Scotland, Wales was made up of a series of small independent regions. Each region was ruled by a leader known as a *tywysog*, or prince. These princedoms were first united by Llywelyn Fawr ('the Great', reigned 1218–40), prince of Gwynedd. His son Dafydd became the second prince of Wales until his death in 1246, when Llywelyn Yr Ail ('the Last') inherited the title.

Caernarfon Castle was the birthplace of the first English prince to take the title prince of Wales. The current prince, Charles, was invested there in 1969.

In 1586 the English historian William Camden described the taking of office, or **investiture**, of a prince of Wales in 1343:

'King Edward the Third first created his eldest sonne Edward surnamed the Blacke Prince... Prince of Wales by solemne investure, with a cap of estate and Coronet set on his head, a gold ring put upon his finger... with the assent of Parliament.'

This is a Victorian impression of what Edward I may have looked like. A warlike king, Edward is shown holding a sword.

DETECTIVE WORK

The current prince of Wales was born in 1948 and formally took the title in 1969. Find out more about Prince Charles, his life, his family and his work on www. princeofwales.gov.uk

Edward I of England (reigned 1272–1307) was a warrior king who aimed to unite both Wales and Scotland under his rule. Two years after he became king, he summoned Llywelyn Yr Ail to him. Llywelyn refused, as that would suggest that Edward was his master. In response, in 1277 Edward invaded Wales and defeated Llywelyn, forcing him to swear loyalty to him. Five years later, Llywelyn rebelled, forcing Edward to invade again. On 11 December 1282, Llywelyn was caught and killed on a bridge outside Builth in mid-Wales.

Edward was now master of Wales. He set about building 10 stone castles to serve as administrative centres, army quarters and to guard the coastline, rivers and roads. In 1284, Welsh independence was formally ended by the Statute of Rhuddlan. That same year, while Edward was staying at Caernarfon Castle in north Wales, his wife, Queen Eleanor, gave birth to a son, Edward. When Edward became 17, in 1301, his father made him prince of Wales. Ever since, the English monarch has made his eldest son and heir prince of Wales.

Since Edward, there have been 20 further princes of Wales. Twelve of them later became king, while Charles, the current prince of Wales, still waits to take the throne.

The ostrich-feather badge of Prince Edward the Black Prince (1330–76) is the badge of all the princes of Wales. The motto Ich dien means 'I serve'.

What were the Wars of the Roses?

The Wars of the Roses were a series of civil wars fought between the noble English houses of Lancaster and York. They lasted from 1455 to 1485. They may never have happened if a weak ruler had not come to the throne after a long series of strong kings.

After the death of the last Norman king, Stephen, in 1154, a dynasty known as Plantagenet came to rule England. The Plantagenets were mostly strong leaders. Henry II (reigned 1154–89) created a family empire in France, his son Richard I (reigned 1189–99) went on crusade to the Holy Land, Edward I (reigned 1272–1307) conquered Wales and tried to conquer Scotland, while Edward III (reigned 1327–77) started the Hundred Years War against France.

Edward III's son Richard II, however, was far from strong. He became king in 1377 when he was only 10. In 1397, he had a row with his cousin, Henry Bolingbroke, Duke of Lancaster, and took his lands. In 1399, Henry returned from **exile** abroad and seized the throne, imprisoning Richard in Pontefract Castle, where he died in 1400. Henry, now Henry IV, was the first of three Lancastrian kings. His son, Henry V, won a magnificent victory against the French at Agincourt in 1415. He died leaving his infant son, Henry VI, as king of both England and France.

DETECTIVE WORK
The Wars of the Roses raged on and off for 30 years. But what battles were fought, and who were the most important people? Find out more about this fascinating period of English history at www.warsoftheroses.com

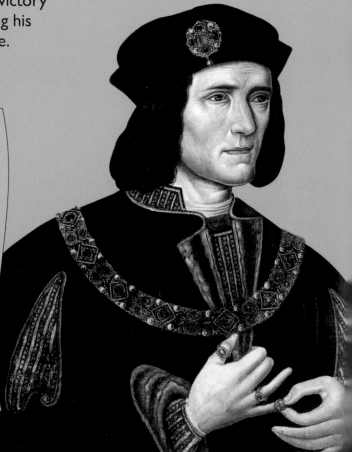

Richard III was the last king of the House of York. Some historians believe that he murdered his young nephews in order to take the throne.

In 1599, William Shakespeare wrote his play *Henry V*. One of its most important scenes takes place on St Crispin's Day, 25 October 1415, the day of Henry's victory at Agincourt. Henry said to his men:

'We few, we happy few, we band of brothers;
For he today that sheds his blood with me
Shall be my brother; be he ne'er so vile,
This day shall gentle his condition:
And gentlemen in England now a-bed
Shall think themselves accursed they were not here,
And hold their manhoods cheap whiles any speaks
That fought with us upon Saint Crispin's day.'

In 1485, the future Henry VII defeated King Richard III at the Battle of Bosworth Field to take the English throne.

Henry VI was kind and gentle but not up to being king. When he fell mentally ill, his cousin, Richard, duke of York, became **Protector**. But the York branch of the family had as much claim to the throne as the Lancastrian branch, and in 1455 took up arms against Henry. The Lancastrians used a red rose as their symbol. The Yorkists used a white rose. The battles between them became known as the Wars of the Roses.

Richard of York was killed in 1460, but in 1461 his son, Edward, defeated Henry VI and became king as Edward IV. His infant son Edward V briefly succeeded him before his uncle, Richard III, became king. In 1485, the Wars of the Roses finally ended when a Lancastrian, Henry Tudor, defeated Richard III and took the throne as Henry VII, the first Tudor king of England.

After seizing the throne back from the Yorkists, Henry VII returned stability to the country. He also founded the powerful Tudor dynasty.

What is being handed to Henry Tudor after the Battle of Bosworth Field?

Why did Henry VIII marry six times?

The one fact that everyone knows about Henry VIII, even if they do not know anything else about him, is that he had six wives. And even for a king, that is a lot of weddings. But why did he marry so often, and what happened to all his wives?

Henry's first wife, Catherine of Aragon, was the daughter of Ferdinand and Isabella, King and Queen of Spain. Henry was not meant to marry her at all, as in 1501 she had already married his elder brother, Prince Arthur. But Arthur died in 1503, and when Henry eventually became king in 1509, he married Catherine. The couple had a daughter, the future Queen Mary I, but no son, and Henry was desperate for a male heir to secure the **succession** to the throne.

Henry decided that the lack of a male heir was punishment from God for marrying his former sister-in-law. He tried to get the Pope – the head of the **Roman Catholic Church** – to **annul** or cancel the marriage. When the Pope refused, Henry got **Parliament** to declare him supreme head of the Church of England. This was the start of the English Reformation that saw England become a **Protestant** nation.

Henry VIII was the second monarch of the House of Tudor. He succeeded his father, Henry VII, in 1509.

DETECTIVE WORK

The names of Henry's three wives called Catherine are sometimes spelt in different ways. Find out more about them and Henry's other three wives at www. tudorhistory.org/wives

In 1533, Henry divorced Catherine and married Anne Boleyn, who gave birth to a daughter, the future Elizabeth I. Again, his wife produced no son and so, in 1536, Henry had Anne executed on charges of **treason**. He then married his third wife, Jane Seymour, who in 1537 gave birth to a son, the future Edward VI. Sadly, Jane died soon after childbirth, leaving Henry with a male heir and two daughters, but no wife.

In 1540, Henry wed for the fourth time. Before he married his new wife, the German princess Anne of Cleves, Henry had only seen a beautiful portrait of her. Unfortunately, he took an instant dislike to his wife's looks when he met her, and the marriage was annulled after seven months. Within three weeks, Henry had married his fifth wife, Catherine Howard, but she had a string of lovers. When Henry found out, she was executed for treason. In 1543, Henry married for the sixth time. His last wife, Catherine Parr, had already been married and widowed twice, and was seen as an ideal stepmother to his three children. The marriage was successful and lasted until Henry himself died in 1547.

After rejecting Anne of Cleves, Henry felt sorry for her and gave her the title 'the king's sister'.

Catherine Parr married Henry when she was 31.

The Act of Supremacy passed by Parliament in 1534 stated that Henry VIII was:

'the only supreme head on earth of the Church in England.'

The Act also said that the English crown shall enjoy:

'all honours, dignities, pre-eminences, jurisdictions, privileges, authorities, immunities, profits, and commodities to the said dignity.'

Other than during the short reign of Mary I (1553–58), every English and British monarch since Henry has been head of the English Church.

🐾 The artist Holbein has focused on something in his portrait of Anne of Cleves. What is it?

Who united the crowns?

Despite constant English invasions and attempts to seize or control the Scottish throne, England and Scotland remained separate until the start of the seventeenth century. When their crowns were finally united in 1603, the event was strangely peaceful.

Although she received numerous offers of marriage, Elizabeth I of England (reigned 1558–1603) never married and had no children. Her heir was her cousin, Mary Queen of Scots. Upon Mary's execution in 1587, the succession passed to her son, James VI of Scotland.

King James wanted to be king of Great Britain, but Parliament raised all sorts of objections. In 1603 he made this speech to Parliament:

'What God hath conjoined let no man separate. I am the husband and the whole isle is my lawful wife; I am the head and it is my body; I am the shepherd and it is my flock. I hope therefore that no man will think that I, a Christian King under the Gospel, should be a polygamist and husband to two wives; that I being the head should have a divided or monstrous body or that being the shepherd to so fair a flock should have my flock parted in two.'

DETECTIVE WORK

The execution of a former queen was a rare and tragic event. Using books from your school or local library, read about the death of Mary Queen of Scots.

James was a talented scholar who wrote books on philosophy and politics.

When Queen Elizabeth I finally died on 24 March 1603, James was proclaimed king in London later the same day, becoming James I of England and James VI of Scotland. He was the first of the Stuart line of kings.

Although James was now king of both countries, Scotland and England remained separate from each other. Each kingdom had its own Parliament, laws and Protestant Church. This situation continued until, in 1707, both the English and Scottish Parliaments passed an Act of Union. This set up a single Parliament for both countries and a single kingdom, known as the United Kingdom of Great Britain.

Elsewhere in the British Isles, England had absorbed Wales in 1284 and formally united the two countries between 1536 and 1543. Ireland had largely been under English control since Henry II invaded it in 1171, but did not unite with the rest of the country until its own Act of Union in 1800.

At this point, the official name of the country changed to the United Kingdom of Great Britain and Ireland. It kept that name until the 26 counties in the south of Ireland won independence in 1922, leaving just six Northern Irish counties in the Union. The country was then renamed again as the United Kingdom of Great Britain and Northern Ireland, the name it has today.

In the painting of James (opposite) he is wearing something special round his knee. What is it?

Scotland again got its own Parliament in 1999. This is the new Parliament building in Holyrood, Edinburgh.

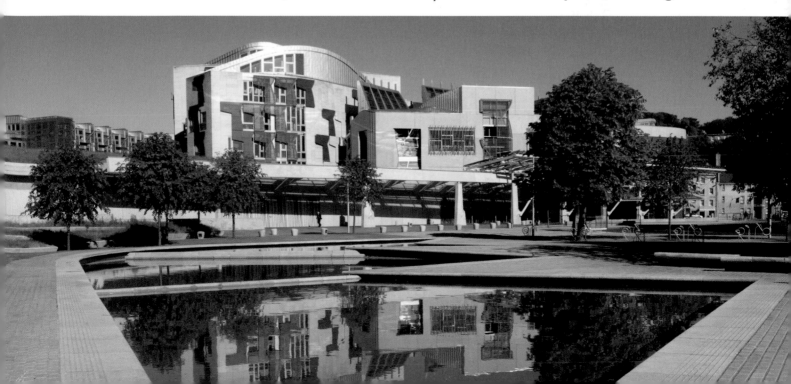

Why did a king lose his head?

Ever since the four nations of the British Isles were first formed, they have separately and then together been ruled by kings, queens or princes. There has been one exception, however. For in 1649 the king was executed and Britain became a republic.

Charles is shown with the ancient crown of England. After his execution, Oliver Cromwell had it melted down.

A republic is a country where the head of state is not a hereditary monarch but an ordinary person who is chosen by the people. As we have seen, most countries in the world today are republics, with only a handful of monarchies surviving. But in the mid-1600s, when Britain lost its king, republics were very rare. Britain's was one of the first.

When James VI of Scotland came south to become James I of England in 1603, he brought with him an idea known as the Divine Right of Kings. He believed that God had given him the right to rule and that he answered to God alone for what he did – not to the people or their Parliament. This caused some problems for James but far greater problems for his son Charles I (reigned 1625–49). He was a clever man but he was quarrelsome. Charles also clashed with Parliament, refusing to summon it to a meeting from 1629 to 1640 and trying to rule by himself.

DETECTIVE WORK

Charles I is the only British king to have been put on trial and then executed. You can find out more about his trial and execution at www.british-civil-wars.co.uk/glossary/trial-king-charles.htm

Charles was beheaded in public by an axeman.

The king's allies were called Cavaliers and wore feathered hats. Supporters of Parliament were called Roundheads.

In 1642, Charles tried to arrest five members of Parliament who opposed him. The result was a civil war that led to Parliament's victory in 1648. Charles refused to negotiate with Parliament or with its army led by Oliver Cromwell, and so in January 1649 Charles was put on trial for treason. He was found guilty and on 30 January executed on a scaffold in Whitehall, London, in front of a crowd.

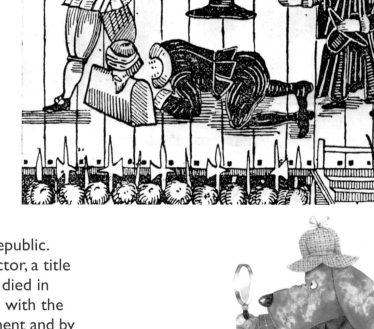

For the next 11 years, Britain was a republic. Oliver Cromwell became Lord Protector, a title inherited by his son Richard when he died in 1658. But people soon became fed up with the harsh rule of this new type of government and by 1660 many wanted the monarchy back. Charles I's son, also Charles, was asked back from exile in the Netherlands and on 25 May landed at Dover. Within a year he was crowned King Charles II (reigned 1660–85). The British republic had ended and the country became a monarchy again.

🐾 **In the picture above, what did Charles rest his head on before being executed?**

When did the kings speak German?

Throughout the sixteenth and seventeenth centuries, religion caused huge political rows in Britain. The Reformation or religious revolution that swept Europe in the early 1500s led to the creation of new Protestant churches that broke away from the Roman Catholic Church. Protestant churches were set up in England and Wales, and in Scotland, although Ireland remained mostly Roman Catholic.

Both Elizabeth I and James I were Protestants, and so were Charles I and Charles II, but both were suspected of supporting Roman Catholicism. Charles II's brother, James II (reigned 1685–88), became a Catholic in the 1660s and, once on the throne, tried to restore the Catholic faith to Britain. Religion was very important, as most British people valued their Protestant beliefs and did not want the country to become Catholic again.

George I was thought cold and unfeeling by many people in Britain, perhaps because he could not speak English to them. His mother, Sophia, thought differently:

'explaining to those who regarded him as cold and overserious that he could be jolly, that he took things to heart, that he felt deeply and sincerely and was more sensitive than he cared to show.'

DETECTIVE WORK

The Hanoverians were the latest in a long line of English royal families that came from abroad. The Normans were French, the Stuarts Scottish, and William III Dutch. Find out more about this German family and its monarchs on www.royal.gov.uk/HistoryoftheMonarchy/KingsandQueensofthe UnitedKingdom/TheHanoverians

Under George III, Britain expanded its empire, despite losing the American colonies.

As a result, James was chased off the throne in 1689 and his place taken by his Protestant daughter, Mary, who ruled jointly with her Dutch Protestant husband, William III.

In 1701, the English Parliament passed the Act of Settlement. This law stated that Britain would never again be ruled by a Catholic monarch and laid out the order of the succession to the throne to ensure a Protestant monarch if William or his heir, Mary's sister, Anne, died without children. Anne (reigned 1702–14) became queen on William's death but, despite giving birth to numerous children, none of them survived her.

So, on Queen Anne's death the crown passed over the claims of 51 Catholics and went to the Protestant great-grandson of James I. His name was George and he was a German prince from Hanover. Born and brought up in Germany, he spoke no English. At the age of 54, he unexpectedly became king of Great Britain, as well as ruler of Hanover.

George I is shown here in the robes of an English knight. He became king in 1714 without ever having been to England.

George I was succeeded by his son George II in 1727, another German-speaking monarch born in Hanover. He spoke some English, although with a heavy Germany accent, as did his grandson and successor George III (reigned 1760–1820), who was born in England. Indeed, all six Hanoverian monarchs, from George I to Victoria, married Germans and spoke German as a first language or English with a strong German accent.

🐾 **What are these two kings wearing that was fashionable in the eighteenth century?**

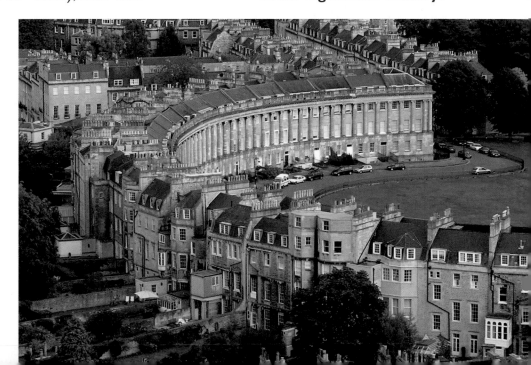

The Royal Crescent in Bath, begun in 1767, is an example of the elegant Georgian style.

Which monarch reigned the longest?

On 22 January 1901, Queen Victoria died at Osborne House on the Isle of Wight. She was 81 and had been on the throne of Great Britain for 63 years and 7 months, the longest reign of any British monarch. But who was this long-lived woman, and how did she achieve such fame?

Victoria was the only daughter of the duke of Kent and his German-speaking wife, Princess Victoria of Saxe-Coburg-Saalfield. She had little chance of succeeding to the throne, as her father was only the fourth son of George III (1760–1820), and his three elder brothers were all still alive. But the duke died within a week of George III in 1820 and his three older brothers died soon after him. None of these three had any surviving legitimate heirs. Only Victoria was still alive. On 20 June 1837, at the age of only 18, Victoria therefore became queen.

Victoria came to the throne just as Britain was becoming the world's first industrial nation. The country was increasingly rich, and was building its own powerful empire around the world.

Victoria and Albert visited the Balmoral estate in 1848 and enjoyed their stay so much that, in 1852, they bought it.

🐾 Balmoral is built in the Scottish castle style. What are the features of this style?

DETECTIVE WORK

Victoria sat on the throne for a record 63 years, 7 months and 2 days. Our present queen, Elizabeth, came to the throne on 6 February 1952. Can you work out the exact date on which she will break Victoria's record?

In 1851 Victoria opened the Great Exhibiton in London. It displayed new industrial inventions from all over the empire.

At home, the country was run by a prime minister. Victoria was more of a figurehead than a ruling monarch, so there was little danger that she would be **overthrown** or executed, as some of her more unpopular ancestors had been.

A far greater personal risk arose after her marriage in 1840 to her cousin, Prince Albert of Saxe-Coburg and Gotha, two small **duchies** in Germany. Victoria had a very happy marriage and bore nine children at a time when childbirth was risky for any woman. Yet Victoria easily survived the difficulties of childbirth. What she did not survive so well was the death of Albert in 1861, aged only 42. Victoria was deeply upset and went into **mourning**, hiding herself away in her royal palaces at Windsor and Balmoral in Scotland. She wore black for the rest of her life and did not appear in public for years. This led many people to ask whether Britain might not be better off ending the monarchy and setting up a republic instead.

Victoria was eventually tempted out of retirement by her prime minister Benjamin Disraeli, who had her created empress of India in 1876. Her Golden Jubilee in 1887 and her Diamond Jubilee in 1897 were huge national celebrations that showed Victoria how popular she was.

This photograph of Victoria was taken for her Diamond Jubilee in 1897, when she was 78 years old.

Why is the royal family named after a castle?

When Queen Victoria died in 1901, her son Prince Albert Edward, who took the title King Edward VII, became king. As the son of Prince Albert, he took his father's surname and so became the first monarch of the new royal house of Saxe-Coburg-Gotha. When Edward died in 1910, his son King George V kept the surname. It might have been royal, but within a few years this German mouthful of a name became a national embarrassment.

There were probably only a handful of people in Britain who knew where in the world Saxe-Coburg and Gotha actually were. These two small duchies were in central Germany, sandwiched between Bavaria in the south and Prussia in the north. They had become part of the united German empire in 1871. Their ruler, the duke of Albany, was the English-born grandson of Queen Victoria.

DETECTIVE WORK

Windsor Castle has been a royal residence since the mid-1300s. Find out more about the historic building that gave its name to a royal family on http://en.wikipedia.org/wiki/Windsor_Castle

Windsor Castle in Berkshire is one of the official residences of the British monarch, along with Buckingham Palace in London.

🐾 **In the picture of Windsor, one part of the castle is much older than the rest. Can you work out which part?**

None of this would have mattered much until, in 1914, Britain and Germany went to war with each other at the start of World War I. Close royal ties existed between the two countries – George V and Kaiser Wilhelm II of Germany were cousins. But far more embarrassing was the royal family name, which was much too Germanic for a monarch leading his country in a bitter war with Germany.

In 1917, George V announced that the royal family would change its name to the more British-sounding name of his favourite residence – Windsor. Other royal family names were also changed. The Prince and Princess of Teck took the surname Cambridge, while the Battenbergs, who had married into the royal family, turned into Mountbattens.

The House of Windsor has remained on the British throne ever since. In January 1936, George V died and was succeeded by his son, Edward VIII. Edward was unmarried, but when he decided to marry an American woman, Wallis Simpson, who had been married and divorced twice, a huge row broke out. Edward was the head of the Church of England, which did not allow divorce. The government of the day also thought Edward's choice of wife was not very suitable. In December 1936, Edward decided to **abdicate**, which means to give up his throne.

In his place, his younger brother, George VI, became king. Unprepared to reign, and with a bad stammer, George VI nevertheless proved to be a popular king who led Britain successfully through World War II. On his death in 1952, his eldest daughter Elizabeth became queen.

Shortly before he died, George V said to his prime minister, Stanley Baldwin, about his son Edward that:

'After I am dead the boy will ruin himself in 12 months.'

His forecast was correct.

Queen Elizabeth II is the UK's present monarch. She is also queen of 15 other countries in the Commonwealth – a group of nations that were once part of the British empire.

Your project

By now you should have collected lots of information about the British monarchy and its fascinating history. This is the time to think about the sort of project you might like to do.

You could write a profile of one of the colourful monarchs that have sat on the thrones of England or Scotland over the past 1,200 years. Try writing a short biography or life story of one of them, perhaps setting out events from their point of view and explaining why they acted in the way they did. Or, you could instead write about what it was like to work for a monarch, perhaps as a courtier, servant or soldier. Remember, it is your project, so choose someone who interests you.

Alternatively, you could organise your own debate about the monarchy. Set out the reasons why it is a good idea to have a monarch, and then list the arguments that could be made against it. You can contribute to the debate on one side or other, or summon evidence from a king or queen to support the royal case. You could even hear evidence from a republican like Oliver Cromwell. Think about why Britain still has a monarchy when so many countries are republics, and why our monarchy has survived this long when so many others have been swept away by history.

This portrait of the future Elizabeth I was painted when she was a young princess in 1547. Her reign (1558–1603) is sometimes called a 'Golden Age', when literature and the arts flourished in England.

Oliver Cromwell did not want a fancy portrait. He famously told the artist to paint him 'warts and all'.

Project presentation

- Research your project well. Use the Internet and your local or school library. Is there a nearby society, museum or historical site related to your project? Many of these will also have their own Internet site.

- If you were a time-travelling journalist and could interview your featured monarch, what questions would you ask them?

- Are there any castles or grand estates in your area? Do any of them have a royal history? See if you can visit them and find out which kings or queens are connected with them.

- If you are setting up a debate, what questions need to be asked and answered before a conclusion can be reached?

In mid-June, troops mark the monarch's birthday in a parade known as 'Trooping the Colour'.

Glossary

abdicate To give up the throne voluntarily.

annul To declare a law or marriage to be invalid.

CE 'Common Era.' Used to signify years since the believed birth of Jesus.

civil war A war between two sides in the same country.

coronation The ceremony of crowning a monarch.

crown The ornamental headdress of a monarch. The crown also represents the monarchy.

duchies The areas of land ruled by dukes.

dynasty A series of monarchs from the same royal family.

empire A collection of countries united under the rule of one monarch, known as an emperor.

exile The time a person spends living abroad because they have been banned from their own country.

figurehead A person with a symbolic role but no power.

heir A person who succeeds to the property of another on that person's death.

hereditary system The passing down of a royal title, or office or land, through the generations of a family.

house A royal family, such as the Tudors or Windsors.

illegitimate A person born to unmarried parents.

investiture The formal giving of a title to someone.

kingdom A country ruled over by a monarch.

monarch A king or queen.

monarchy A form of government with a king or queen as head of state.

mourning A period of grieving following the death of a loved one.

overlord A supreme lord or master.

overthrow To remove a ruler by force.

pagan A person who does not belong to any of the world's main religions.

parliament A law-making authority composed of elected members.

prince The son of a king and queen. A daughter is known as a princess.

princedom A country or region ruled by a prince.

Protector The person who handles royal matters when the monarch is absent.

Protestant A Christian person who does not accept the supremacy of the Roman Catholic Church.

republic A system of government in which people elect their head of state.

Roman Catholic Church The main Christian Church in western Europe, led by the Pope in Rome.

succession The order in which one monarch follows another.

throne The chair on which a monarch sits. The throne also represents the monarchy.

treason A crime against the monarch or country.

Answers

Page 4:   British monarchs wear a crown and special robes. At their coronation they also hold a sceptre, orb, sword and other symbols of their power.

Page 6:   They were buried with goods that represented their wealth and position, such as jewellery and weapons.

Page 9:   Their collars and cuffs are made of ermine, an expensive fur used only on royal robes.

Page 11:   William is carrying a falcon, which was used for hunting.

Page 15:   Henry Tudor is being handed the crown from Richard III's helmet. It was found in a hawthorn bush on the battlefield.

Page 17:   Holbein focused on her beautiful dress, instead of her face.

Page 19:   James is wearing a garter (a type of suspender), a symbol of English medieval knighthood.

Page 21:   Charles's head rested on a block.

Page 23:   Both kings are wearing wigs.

Page 24:   Scottish castles have a large keep (castle-like tower) with small, pointed turrets.

Page: 27:   The tower to the left is much older. It was built on a 'motte', or a man-made hill, in Norman times and later covered in stone. See also the castle on page 10.

Further Information

Books to read
Kings and Queens: A Royal History of England and Scotland by Plantagenet Somerset Fry (Dorling Kindersley 1997)
Horrible Histories: Cruel Kings and Mean Queens by Terry Deary (Hippo 1995)

Websites
www.royal.gov.uk
www.britannia.com/history/h6f.html
www.historyonthenet.com/Monarchy/monarchymain.htm
Note to parents and teachers: Every effort has been made by the publishers to ensure that these websites are suitable for children. However, because of the nature of the Internet, it is impossible to guarantee that the contents of these sites will not be altered. We strongly advise that Internet access is supervised by a responsible adult.

Places to visit
Buckingham Palace, London SW1A 1AA
Windsor Castle, Windsor, Berkshire SL4 1NJ
Edinburgh Castle, Castle Hill, Edinburgh EH1 2NG
Caernarfon Castle, Castle Ditch, Caernarfon LL55 2AY

Index

Numbers in **bold** refer to pictures and captions

abbeys **5**, **8**
abdication 27
Agincourt, Battle of 14
Alfred the Great 7, **7**
Anglo-Saxons 6
Anne, Queen 23
Anne of Cleves 17, **17**

castles and palaces **4**, **10**, **12**, 13, **24**, **26**
Catholic Church 16, 22, 23
Charles I 20–21, **20**, **21**, 22
Charles II 21, 22
Charles, Prince of Wales **12**, 13
civil wars 8, 14, 21
coronation 4, **5**
Cromwell, Oliver **20**, 21, **28**

Ecgberht 7
Edward I 9, 13, **13**
Edward VIII 27
Elizabeth I 17, 18–19, 22, **28**
Elizabeth II **1**, 25, 27, **27**
England 5, 6–7, **6**, 18
execution 21, **21**

George I 22, 23, **23**
George III **22**, 23, 24
George V 26, 27

Hanoverians 22–23
Harold 11, **11**
Hastings, Battle of 11
Henry V 14
Henry VII 15, **15**
Henry VIII 16–17, **16**

Ireland 19, 22

James I 18–19, **18**, 20, 22
James II 22, 23

Kenneth MacAlpin 8, **8**

Lancaster, House of 14, 15
Llywelyn Yr Ail 12, 13

Malcolm II 8
Mary Queen of Scots 18
monarchy 4–5, 21

Normans 10–11

parliament **19**, 20–21
Parr, Catherine 17, **17**
Plantagenets 14
prime ministers 4, 25
Protestant Church 16, 22

republics 5, 20–21, 25
Richard III **14**, 15, **15**
Robert Bruce 9, **9**

Saxe-Coburg-Gotha 26
Scotland 5, 8–9, 18–19, **19**

Victoria, Queen 24–25, **25**
Vikings 7–8, **7**, 10, 11

Wales 12–13, 19
Wallace, William 9, **9**
Wars of the Roses 14–15
William and Mary 23
William the Conqueror 8, 10–11, **10**, **11**
Windsor, House of 26–27

York, House of 14, 15